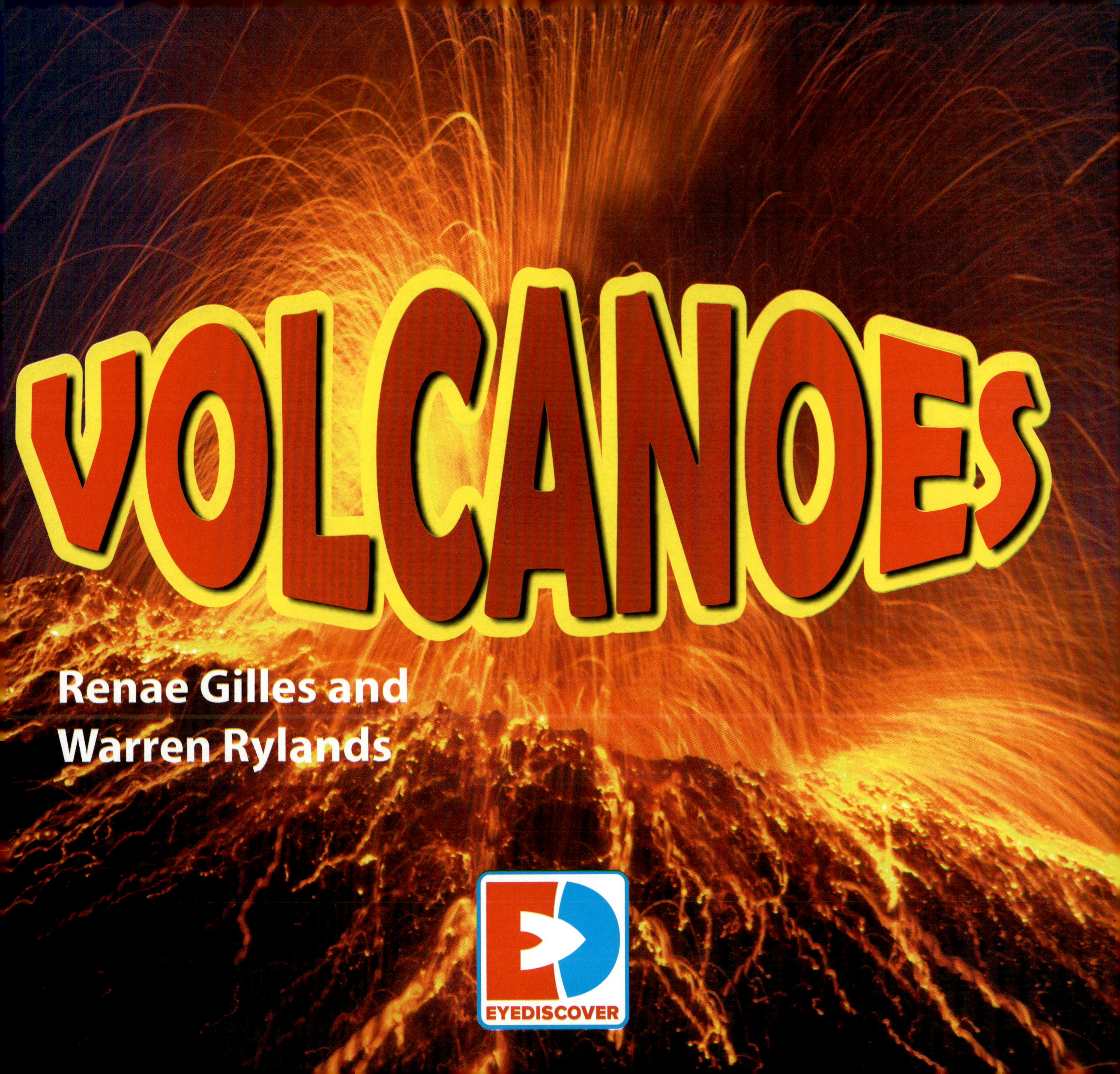
VOLCANOES
Renae Gilles and
Warren Rylands
EYEDISCOVER

Go to www.eyediscover.com and enter this book's unique code.

BOOK CODE

AVE88253

EYEDISCOVER brings you optic readalongs that support active learning.

Published by AV² by Weigl
350 5th Avenue, 59th Floor New York, NY 10118
Website: www.eyediscover.com

Library of Congress Control Number: 2018951110

ISBN 978-1-4896-8023-5 (hardcover)

Printed in the United States of America
in Brainerd, Minnesota
1 2 3 4 5 6 7 8 9 0 22 21 20 19 18

082018
120917

Project Coordinator: John Willis
Designer: Mandy Christiansen

Weigl acknowledges Alamy, Getty Images, and Shutterstock as the primary image suppliers for this title.

EYEDISCOVER provides enriched content, optimized for tablet use, that supplements and complements this book. EYEDISCOVER books strive to create inspired learning and engage young minds in a total learning experience.

Watch
Video content brings each page to life.

Browse
Thumbnails make navigation simple.

Read
Follow along with text on the screen.

Listen
Hear each page read aloud.

Your EYEDISCOVER Optic Readalongs come alive with...

Audio
Listen to the entire book read aloud.

Video
High resolution videos turn each spread into an optic readalong.

OPTIMIZED FOR
- ✔ TABLETS
- ✔ WHITEBOARDS
- ✔ COMPUTERS
- ✔ AND MUCH MORE!

In this book, you will learn about

- how they look
- where they are
- what they do

and much more!

A volcano is a mountain that sits on top of melted rock.

Volcanoes erupt when melted rock and gases build up.

When a volcano erupts, it spews lava, rocks, gases, and ash.

An eruption can make earthquakes, floods, and giant ocean waves.

Most volcanoes form on land. Some volcanoes form under the water.

Some volcanoes can be tall and steep. Others are short and wide.

There are three kinds of volcanoes. Active volcanoes are volcanoes that can erupt again.

Dormant volcanoes have not erupted for a long time. Extinct volcanoes will probably never erupt again.

Volcanoes can create new land. Soon, plants can begin to grow there.

VOLCANOES BY THE NUMBERS

There are **1,900** **active volcanoes** on Earth.

More than **90 percent** of volcanoes are around the **Pacific Ocean**.

The **largest** volcano on Earth is Hawai'i's **Mauna Loa**.

About
350 million
people live by an
active volcano.

Lava can reach a
temperature of
2,280°
Fahrenheit.
(1,249° Celsius)

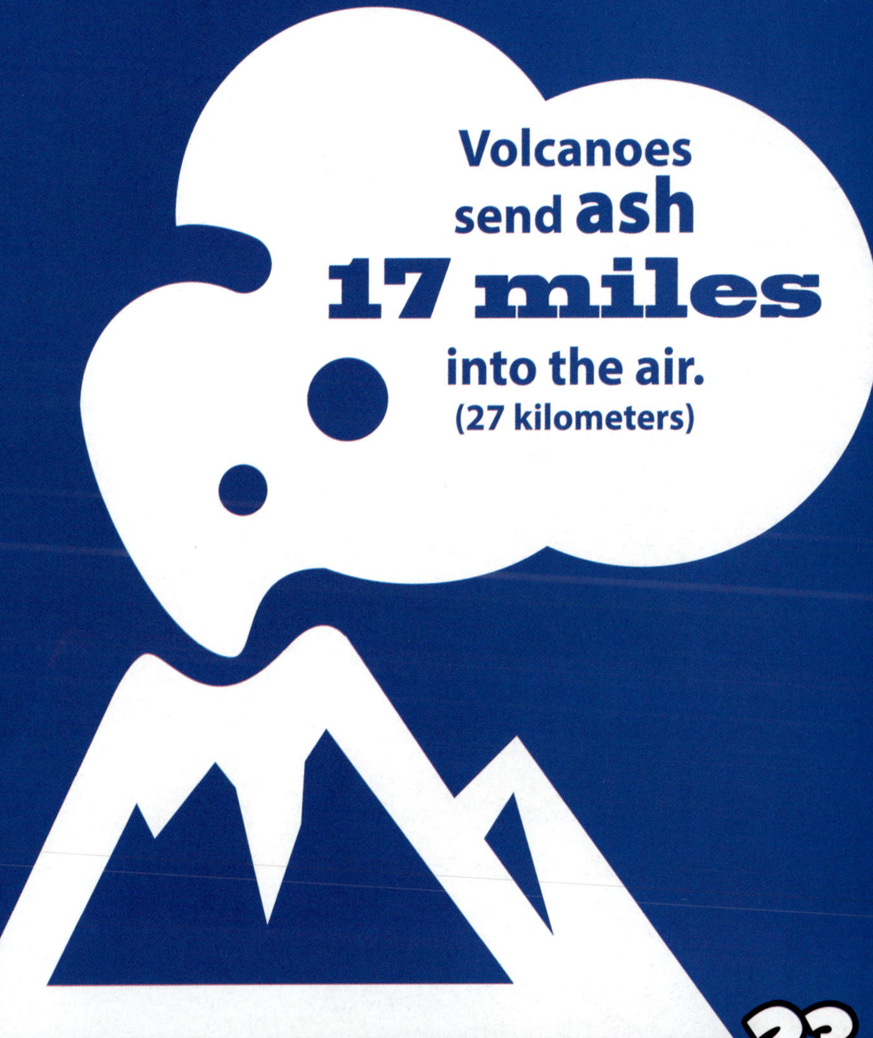

KEY WORDS

Research has shown that as much as 65 percent of all written material published in English is made up of 300 words. These 300 words cannot be taught using pictures or learned by sounding them out. They must be recognized by sight. This book contains 38 common sight words to help young readers improve their reading fluency and comprehension. This book also teaches young readers several important content words, such as proper nouns. These words are paired with pictures to aid in learning and improve understanding.

Page	Sight Words First Appearance
4	a, is, mountain, of, on, that
7	and, up, when
8	it
11	an, can, make
12	land, most, some, the, under, water
15	are, be, others
16	again, kinds, there, three
19	for, have, long, never, not, time, will
20	grow, new, plants, soon, to

Page	Content Words First Appearance
4	rock, volcano
7	gases, erupt
8	ash, lava
11	earthquakes, floods, waves
16	active volcanoes
19	dormant volcanoes, extinct volcanoes

Watch
Video content brings each page to life.

Browse
Thumbnails make navigation simple.

Read
Follow along with text on the screen.

Listen
Hear each page read aloud.

Go to www.eyediscover.com and enter this book's unique code.

BOOK CODE

AVE88253